TAXES AT WORK

A CITIZEN'S GUIDE

Published in the United States of America by Cherry Lake Publishing
Ann Arbor, Michigan
www.cherrylakepublishing.com

Content Adviser: Austin McCoy, Doctoral Candidate in History at the University of Michigan
Reading Adviser: Marla Conn MS, Ed., Literacy specialist, Read-Ability, Inc.

Photo Credits: © Joseph Sohm/Shutterstock, cover, 1, 8; © Leonard Zhukovsky/Shutterstock, 5; © Duncan Walker/istock, 6; © bikeriderlondon/Shutterstock, 11; © easyshutter/Shutterstock, 12; © Celso Diniz/Shutterstock, 14; © lumen-digital/Shutterstock, 16; © Dmitry Kalinovsky/Shutterstock, 19; © Voronin76/Shutterstock, 21; © Jane Rix/Shutterstock, 22; © Lisa F. Young/Shutterstock, 25; © XiXinXing/Shutterstock, 26; © Emolaev Alexander/Shutterstock, 28

Library of Congress Cataloging-in-Publication Data
CIP data has been filed and is available at catalog.loc.gov.

Cherry Lake Publishing would like to acknowledge the work of the Partnership for 21st Century Learning. Please visit *www.p21.org* for more information.

Printed in the United States of America
Corporate Graphics

ABOUT THE AUTHOR

Wil Mara is an award-winning and best-selling author of more than 150 books, many of which are educational titles for young readers. Further information about his work can be found at www.wilmara.com.

TABLE OF CONTENTS

CHAPTER 1

Taking Government for Granted

It's easy to take your government for granted. If we need help in an emergency, we simply dial 911 and the police or firefighters head to your house right away. If we need to go somewhere, we hop on a bus, a subway, or a highway. When we retire, the government provides us with health insurance if we don't already have our own. And when we turn on the faucet, clean water comes out.

All these things and many more have been there throughout our lives, so we tend to forget the hard work that goes into providing them. There was a time in American history when such services were little more than a dream. They developed over time as people needed them, and the funds that make them possible come from **taxes** and other fees. Where do the various government bodies get those funds? From *you*!

Police officers are employed by state and local government.

In the Boston Tea Party, colonists threw tea overboard to protest against the high taxes on it.

The American Revolution (1775—1783) was fought partly in protest against taxes. The colonists were still being taxed by England, even though no one in the British government had their interests in mind. "No taxation without representation!" became the colonists' motto.

The first **income tax** in the United States was imposed in the 1860s in order to fund the Civil War. Once the war was over, some lawyers became concerned about the constitutional legality of continuing to take a portion of people's earnings. In 1913, an amendment was added to the Constitution—the 16th Amendment—making an income tax legal.

Life and Career Skills

It's against the law to avoid paying taxes. But sometimes people refuse to pay them, because they don't like how the money is being used. Do you think people should ever break laws to support their beliefs? Why or why not?

Taxes keep firehouses running and pay firefighters' salaries.

The government provides all kinds of public services, such as fire-fighting. Government officials hire and train the firefighters, build and maintain the firehouses, buy trucks and equipment, and cover medical bills when firefighters are injured. The government takes care of a lot of things that most of us never even know about.

CHAPTER 2

Where the Money Goes

The inventor and **politician** Benjamin Franklin said, "In this world, nothing is certain but death and taxes." Whether we like them or not (and for the majority of people, it's "not"), taxes need to be paid. The government has the legal right to collect them, per Article 1, Section 8 of the Constitution. It says: "The Congress shall have power to lay and collect taxes, duties, imposts and excises, [and] to pay the debts and provide for the common defense and general welfare of the United States."

Taxation is the main method by which the federal government—which is the national level of government in the United States—raises money. The biggest source within this category is known as income tax, which is based on how much money a person makes in the course of a year. Generally

People need to file the previous year's taxes by each April 15th.

Some tax money goes towards maintaining roads.

speaking, your taxes grow along with your income, which leads to another famous saying: "The more you make, the more they take!" Tax money is sent to the federal government's Internal Revenue Service (IRS), a bureau of the United States Treasury Department. In 2015 alone, the IRS collected over $3 trillion!

One of the most important duties of the federal government is maintaining a strong military—army, navy, air force, marines, and others. A great deal of tax revenue pays for this necessity. It is used to supply equipment such as guns, ships, tanks, and airplanes. It pays for soldiers' training, uniforms, meals, and beds. It also pays for the military academies in West Point, New York; Annapolis, Maryland; and Colorado Springs, Colorado. And since the terrorist attacks on September 11, 2001, the amount of money devoted to national defense has increased dramatically.

Federal taxes pay for critical services that we rarely see but definitely need. An example of this is the services provided by the Centers for Disease Control and Prevention (CDC). The people who work for the CDC identify and then study new diseases as

Life and Career Skills

Leadership is a quality found in many of America's greatest politicians. Leadership is the ability of one person to get others to follow them. And when it comes to spending tax money, some government employees have to decide what gets ***funded*** *and what doesn't. If, for example, there are three projects that all seem important, but there's only enough tax money to pay for two, how do you decide which one will be set aside? A good leader is not only able to make these tough calls but also willing to take on the responsibility of doing so—even if some people will be disappointed. What kind of projects in your town do you feel need the most attention? Which would you fund with the taxpayers' hard-earned money? And which would you set aside? Explain your reasoning.*

NASA also benefits from tax dollars.

they arise and search for ways to keep them away from the public. Another important government agency is the Department of the Treasury. It is responsible for not only printing money but also tracking down **counterfeiters**. Federal taxes cover the salaries of all major positions in the federal government, such as the president, members of Congress, and the justices of the Supreme Court.

Tax dollars keep Medicare and Medicaid afloat. Medicare is a health insurance program for citizens age 65 and over. Doctor visits, hospital stays, x-rays, and other tests are all covered. Medicaid is a health insurance program for citizens younger than

65 who have low incomes and few resources. Many of the people who benefit from Medicaid are children.

Federal taxes are often used to fund projects that neither ordinary citizens nor large, successful companies could pay for, such as space exploration. The National Aeronautics and Space Administration (NASA) was formed in 1958, and some of its achievements have been remarkable. In 1969, for example, NASA succeeded in putting humans on the moon. That was a major moment not just in American history but in *human* history—and it could not have been done without tax money.

Life and Career Skills

Another way to get involved in the governing of your community is to take part in a political ***campaign****. During any campaign, the issue of taxes always comes up. The main question in the mind of most voters will be, "Are my taxes going to go up again?" No politician wants to be the bearer of bad news, but the truth is that tax money still needs to keep flowing into the local government so that expenses can be covered and programs funded. How would you, as someone on the candidate's campaign team, think such a question would best be handled? When the candidate turned to you for advice, what would you tell him or her?*

United States embassies, like this one in Germany, are important resources for Americans traveling abroad.

The federal government manages our national parks. These include famous places like the Grand Canyon, Yellowstone, and the Everglades. The National Park Service (NPS) also oversees national landmarks such as the Statue of Liberty and Mount Rushmore. In addition, the NPS maintains locations with historical significance, such the New Jersey laboratory of inventor Thomas Edison and the Illinois home of Abraham Lincoln.

Since the federal government represents the United States to the rest of the world, federal tax dollars pay for the upkeep of American **embassies** in other nations. There are U.S. embassies in more than 150 countries, and in some places there are numerous offices. Tax money funds special hospitals for military veterans. It maintains the National Archives, which houses important documents such as the Constitution. Once every decade, the government must count every single person in the nation, a practice known as the national census. This involves millions of workers and costs billions of dollars—tax dollars.

CHAPTER 3

State and Local Taxes

While the federal government plays a significant role in most Americans' lives, state and local governments often have just as much impact, if not more.

States and cities get some of their financing from the federal government. However, other sources of funding are usually needed as well, so many states have a state income tax—money its citizens must pay on their income. States often have a sales tax, too, which is an extra charge for the purchase of certain items. Many states do not, however, tax critical items such as groceries or medicine.

Cities and towns—plus the counties within which they are **incorporated**—have their own powers and responsibilities apart from the state and federal levels of government. These local governmental bodies are concerned with the majority of the

Each city organizes its own garbage collection.

issues and problems you face on a daily basis. For example, they are responsible for making sure that the garbage is collected, clean water flows into your home, and police are on patrol to keep you safe from crime. Local government will likely have the greatest impact on you as you go about your daily life. For example, they fix potholes, stop drunk drivers, and keep archives of birth, death, marriage, and divorce records.

The majority of the money used to support local governments comes from property taxes. This tax is based on the value of the land and structures in a specific location, such as a home, a business, or a farm. Certain places do not have to

21st Century Content

*Don't like the way your local politicians are spending your tax dollars (or your parents' tax dollars)? Then do something about it! America is a **democracy**. And one of the most important rights it provides is the right of citizens to **vote** for the leaders of their government. Voting lets your voice be heard, and it is through voting that ordinary citizens control the way the country runs. Think about it—if you don't like the way your representatives are doing their job, you can vote them out of office! All elected politicians—president, senator, governor, mayor, and beyond—have their jobs because the voters put them there. This is one of the most amazing rights provided by the Constitution.*

Homeowners pay property taxes once per year.

People pay fees to their home state in order to renew their driver's licenses or license plates.

pay property taxes, like hospitals, schools (which are funded by property taxes), and churches. Property taxes are usually collected once a year, the same as income taxes. An assessor studies each property and determines its value, and a percentage of this valuation will be the property tax.

Towns and states have other ways of raising funds, often through fees that may seem relatively small to the citizens but add up to huge numbers. One example is the sale of license plates for cars and trucks. A similar fee is the one citizens have to pay to have their driver's licenses renewed or their cars registered. If you are making improvements to your home, a permit fee will be charged by your local government.

21st Century Content

In 2016, a woman in New York was arrested for not having a license plate on the front of her car. (It isn't required in all states, but it is in New York.) When the police pulled her over, they noticed that something was wrong with her back license plate too. She had painted a piece of cardboard and attached it. "In case you were wondering," the sheriff's office wrote on Facebook, "homemade cardboard license plates are NOT legal."

CHAPTER 4

Key Community Services

The single largest use of tax dollars for most towns can be summed up in one word: schools. From kindergarten through high school, schools need teachers, principals, cafeteria and other staff, books, desks, computers, footballs, maps, lights, heat, and countless items. It is not cheap to run a school!

For most communities, the second-largest expense after schools is emergency services such as police and firefighters. Most citizens hope they never need a police officer or firefighter, but it's a comfort to know they're there. These trained professionals need to be available on a moment's notice, which means communities must employ several shifts of workers. Equipment can be costly, too. Squad cars and fire trucks must be not only purchased but also filled with gas and kept in top running condition.

Public schools rely on taxes to stay funded.

Another significant community expense involves sewage and sanitation. Clean water is something that the average American expects to see every time the faucet is turned on. And when they're done, they expect the wastewater to go down the drain and flow away from their home. Raw sewage can be very dangerous, especially if it seeps into a town's drinking water. Many towns and cities have sewage treatment plants to ensure this doesn't happen.

In large cities, public transportation is an essential service. New York, Washington, and Chicago, for example, have

Many people ride public buses or trains to get to school or work.

well-established and extensive subway and bus services for their citizens—as well as for the many visitors who go to these places every day. Millions of Americans rely on public transportation to travel to and from work. A bus or subway train can move many people at one time while spewing out less air pollution and using less energy than individual cars clogging up the roadways. Commuters also like public transportation because they can check their email or get some work done while somebody else takes care of the driving.

21st Century Content

A portion of tax dollars in many communities is set aside to ensure that the citizens are having fun! Think of that neighborhood park or town swimming pool. The swing set and tetherball get used in the summertime, while the ice rink sees plenty of action during the winter months. A gazebo in the town square provides a place for bands to play as well as a spot for local politicians to address voters. And the baseball diamond sees countless Little League games every year. All of these wonderful parts of everyday life would be impossible if not for money provided by taxes.

Public libraries provide many services for free, funded by tax dollars.

Most communities have libraries with books, videos, and magazines that any citizen with a library card can borrow. The library may also provide meeting rooms for local clubs and special classes. For example, if people want to study their family history, they may be able to take a class about genealogy at the library. The library is, in fact, one of the most beneficial institutions in any town. A world of knowledge is at your fingertips, and it's all free for the taking!

Some towns also have community centers, where people can take classes in everything from yoga to square dancing. A center may also offer low-cost courses in relaxing hobbies such as knitting or painting. It is definitely worth the effort to get on a computer, find your town's home page, and see what kind of community programs are available. Remember—it's your government and your tax money at work, so make the most of it!

Think About It

How much is the sales tax in your state? It might be different for groceries, clothing, medicine, and restaurant food. Look online to find out how different states use money from sales tax.

In the 2010s, many cities and states proposed bills for a "soda tax," which would make consumers pay a little extra money for soda and other sugary drinks. Politicians thought this would encourage people to choose healthier beverages. Soda companies thought this was unfair. What's your opinion? Go online to find out more.

For More Information

BOOKS

Brennan, Linda Crotta. *Understanding Taxes.* Ann Arbor, MI: Cherry Lake Publishing, 2015.

Steinkraus, Kyla. *The Constitution.* Vero Beach, FL: Rourke, 2015.

Winter, Jonah, and Barry Blitt (illustrator). *The Founding Fathers! The Horse-Ridin', Fiddle-Playin', Book-Readin', Gun-Totin' Gentlemen Who Started America.* New York: Atheneum, 2015.

ON THE WEB

IRS—Understanding Taxes: Student Site
https://apps.irs.gov/app/understandingTaxes/student/

Kids.gov—Government
https://kids.usa.gov/government/index.shtml

PBS Kids—The Democracy Project: How Does Government Affect Me?
http://pbskids.org/democracy/my-government/

GLOSSARY

campaign (kam-PAYN) organized action in order to achieve a particular goal

counterfeiters (KOUN-tur-fit-urz) people who create pieces of paper that look like money but are fake

democracy (dih-MAH-kruh-see) a form of government in which the people choose their leaders in elections

embassies (EM-buh-seez) the official places in foreign countries where a government's top representative, called an ambassador, works

funded (FUHN-did) provided with money to use

income tax (IN-kuhm TAKS) a payment made to the government based on the amount of money a person earns

incorporated (in-KOR-puh-ray-tid) included as part of a city or county

politician (pah-lih-TISH-uhn) a person who runs for or holds a government office

taxes (TAKS-iz) money that people and businesses must pay in order to support a government

vote (VOHT) to cast a ballot, making a choice in an election

INDEX